May 1980

A Flower Arranger's Guide to Showing

OVERLEAF
In an English Country Garden
This exhibit had to depict the theme where garden flowers were to predominate.

A graceful bronze figurine of a country wench with outstretched hand is seen to pick a bloom from the profusion of summer flowers and foliages.

The design follows the basic trianglular form using larkspur, foxgloves, and antirrhinums for height, and violas, roses, and astrantia are grouped in the focal area.

The container, which is hidden, is simply a plastic bulb bowl, filled with *Oasis* foam, and covered with chicken wire for extra support.

The whole exhibit is placed on a hessian covered board which completes the country effect

A Flower Arranger's Guide to Showing

Howard Franklin

B T Batsford Limited   London

In affectionate and grateful *memory*
of Hilda Franklin

© Howard Franklin 1979
First published 1979
ISBN 0 7134 3321 3

Filmset in 'Monophoto' Photina by
Servis Filmsetting Limited, Manchester
Printed in Great Britain by
Butler & Tanner Ltd, Frome
for the publishers
B T Batsford Limited
4 Fitzhardinge Street
London W1H 0AH

Contents

Preface by Victoria Holt

To the discerning, sensitive lover of beauty, flowers must play an important part in house decoration. Of course tables, chairs and the kitchen sink are necessities without which we could not comfortably exist; but once we have come under the spell of flowers, they too become necessities – and are a great deal more decorative. The fact is that if we would endow our dwelling with grace and charm, we need flowers.

Like me, you may often have been, somewhat nonplussed when a magnificent array of blooms arrives from someone who wishes to please you; and when you have finished gasping at their beauty you think: 'Yes! But what are they going to look like when *I've* finished with them?' The answer is often: 'A mess', unless, of course, you have a natural gift for display or have studied the art of flower arranging.

I first met Howard Myers Franklin on a ship travelling around the world when he was giving lectures on flower arranging to beginners – and also, of course, to not such beginners. Those lectures were illuminating and intriguing; and he talked to me about the book he was compiling.

Now here it is, completed, and a boon to thousands of those who are dedicated to flowers and wish, as we all must, to improve our presentation of them, to do our best for them and to show them in all their beauty, which is surely what they deserve. For those who are natural artists in flowers here is a wealth of information as to how to display their skill and artistry to the best advantage, to share it and compete with others. As for the uninitiated they can learn why what in their hands is a ragged bunch, which seems to be protesting at being thrust into an unsuitable container, can become a vision of beauty with the deft touches of the expert. There is also much for those who have not yet discovered the fascination of flowers. What we have, in fact, is practical information side by side with a guide to better aesthetic understanding.

Flower arranging is an art and like all arts it must be studied and practised. It is a fascinating and absorbing art; and I doubt it has ever been shown more thoroughly, more interestingly or more lucidly than it has in this book.

Knightsbridge, London 1979   *Victoria Holt*

6

Introduction

This book has been compiled as a guide for all those who wish to attain higher standards in flower arrangement, either for competition or non-competitive exhibition. Although reluctant to lay down rules, it is based on nationally accepted principles which govern floral art classes.

Local Flower Shows are a part of English domestic culture where all meet on common ground, usually the village green. The squire, the farmer, the cottager all come together with a mutual interest in growing plants. Although these shows originally concentrated on horticultural specimens they now include classes in flower arrangement.

Then there are the larger city, county and national shows for those who have perfected their art and wish to match their work at a higher level against other skilled flower arrangers.

Whatever the level of flower arranging, whether it be the local village show, or at the Chelsea Flower Show which is the largest in Great Britain, rules have to apply as a guide for exhibitors, stewards and judges. These rules are not devised to stifle individuality, but to help all those with a love of flowers to display them to their best advantage. If, on reading this book, you discover one new idea, hint or tip; and put it into practise then my efforts will have been worthwhile.

As an international demonstrator, lecturer and judge my work takes me around the world to far away places, invariably 'preaching to the converted' at flower clubs where talents abound and continued interest never fails amongst enthusiastic members. There are, however, still thousands of people who have never heard about floral art, and flower clubs, and the pleasures which await them from growing and arranging flowers. Perhaps this book will come into their hands and so by stimulating their interest in this fascinating art form, they may learn the delights of nature and friendship through flowers.

Howard G L Myers Franklin

The Old Coach House
Dorrington, Shropshire 1979

Acknowledgment

My grateful thanks to my parents for their encouragement and help

Mr and Mrs R Trickett for the use of their beautiful woodland garden

Pat and Carl Jameson for colour photography

Peter Earthy for black and white photography

Mrs D Teasdale for typing the manuscript

Thelma M Nye of Batsfords for her thoughtful guidance

and to my Staff and all my friends for their continued loyal support.

A flower arrangement show is for everyone, whether you are an exhibitor or a spectator, it is the ideal opportunity for those who appreciate the beauty of living plant life to exchange ideas and learn from each other. Everyone must be catered for from the novice to the experienced floral designer.

Basic equipment

Pack in advance to avoid panic or rush using this check list to make sure you have included everything.

Florists scissors   for soft stems and stub wires

Flower cutters   for general use

Secateurs   for all thick woody branches

Wire cutters   for all wire

Knife   for scraping ends of flower stems

Buckets   deep enough for soaking plant material

Polythene sheeting   to work on, which avoids unnecessary mess

Containers   for the actual arrangements

Plasticine   useful for fixing pinholders to containers and also levelling a container if the staging is uneven

Tape measure   to make sure exhibits are the correct size according to the schedule

Plumbers lead   Small pieces of this attached to the back of the rim of a container assist balance and often prevent it toppling over.

Cocktail sticks   to make false stems for fruit or vegetables

Plastic drinking straws   enable the arranger to use hollow stemmed flowers in *Oasis* foam when they are inserted inside the stems

Bases   these are placed under the finished arrangement

Drapes   Fabric which has been pressed and rolled around a cardboard tube for transportation

Reel wire   to anchor wire mesh into the container

Tubes and cones   These hold water and provide added height for plant material. Often they are bound onto sticks or dowel and inserted into the arrangement

Candlecups   Shallow dishes with lump on the underside which fits into the hollow in the top of a candlestick or bottle

Candleholders   Small gadget for holding candles in place. A spike on the underside is placed into *Oasis*

Accessories   Various items allied to any particular exhibit to help the overall design, eg figurines, plates, shells

'Oasis'   or other plastic foam which absorbs water and holds flower material in place in an arrangement

Backgrounds   Often exhibitors use boards for backing their designs in place of drapes

Watering can   Small household type for filling the finished arrangements with water

Atomizer   containing fresh water and two teaspoonsful of *Hibitane*   which is obtainable from chemists and is an antibacteria agent. Finished arrangements should be atomized on completion to keep them fresh

Stub wires   to strengthen and lengthen flower stems. Care must be taken to make sure all wiring is concealed and that plant material is always in water

Drawing pins   to hold drapes in place over backgrounds

Tweezers   for holding very small stems when making miniature arrangements

Ball of wool   green coloured to tie soft or fine stems together

Elastic bands   to anchor wire netting and bind the ends of Narcissus stems if they curl up, or hold rose-buds in a closed state until required

Wire netting   25 mm (1 in.) galvanized mesh for placing over *Oasis* foam as extra support to flower stems

Pin holders   Useful in shallow containers for supporting plant material.

How many entries to attempt

Never be tempted to enter more classes than you feel confident of being able to complete comfortably in the time allowed. Each schedule usually contains a number of competitive classes. Some you will be eligible to enter, others may be limited to advanced arrangers, professional florists, flower clubs or other specific categories.

Decide which classes inspire you most, bearing in mind your own selection of containers and the availability of plant material. If it is your first show then only enter two classes, as more than this can be confusing to an inexperienced exhibitor.

Planning your exhibit

Forward preparation is vital for successful competitive work and it is wise to plan your arrangements well in advance of the show. Never copy from flower arrangement books as Judges are experienced arrangers themselves and will deduct points for lack of originality. It is not always necessary to use rare, exotic or expensive flowers unless the class especially mentions unusual or rare plant material. Often prizes are won by exhibits using only a few blooms or simple garden flowers. It is always helpful if you write down various headings associated with each class you enter and list the items you will require, an example of this method is as follows:

SCHEDULE CLASS TITLE   **By Lake or Stream**

Plant material	Reeds, irises, bulrushes, other aquatic plants
Colour scheme	Tranquil greens and blues
Container	Kidney shaped shallow dish to feature water
Base	Larger than container, kidney shaped board covered with lime green velvet
Mechanics	Large well type pinholder with a small cage of wire netting placed over to support the plant material
Accessories	Small carved wooden heron and pebbles or moss to hide mechanics
Style	Naturalistic
Drape or background	Not required
Research	It is important to make sure all plant material used does in fact grow by either lakes or streams

Conformity to the schedule

The class title should leave you in no doubt as to what type of arrangement is expected. If the schedule says an arrangement in a basket then it is quite obvious that all other types of container should be avoided. This is an obvious example, but sometimes it is not so simple. For example, a class asking for *Glorious Green* – a foliage only arrangement must not contain any flowers, even if they are green in colour, otherwise the entry will be marked 'not according to schedule'. Key words are often used in show schedules which set the mood or style of the class. For example, *Edwardian Elegance, Fascinating Foliage, Baroque Beauty, Monochromatic Moments*. It is wise to look up these key words in a dictionary to confirm their meaning and interpret them accordingly. A stipulation of any kind in the wording must never be ignored. Most shows have a list of definitions in the front of the schedule, or they refer to nationally accepted definitions which can be obtained in booklet form from the show secretary.

The size of the space allowed for your exhibit is always given and the exhibit should stand comfortably within this space, otherwise you may be disqualified. Background heights are normally given, also their colour. It is important that plant material should not protrude above the background height. If you are in any doubt about anything ask the show secretary in advance and avoid disappointment later.

Edwardian Elegance

A period arrangement perfectly portaying the elegance of the Edwardian era.

The design comprises shrub roses, larkspur, and rosa rubrifolia foliage which reflect the hand-painted porcelain urn.

An asymetric triangle is balanced by the small cluster on the base.

The height of the exhibit is approximately one-and-half times the height of the container.

Arrangements made today can only be designed in the 'style' of a past era. Flower arrangers should study not only books but also any available articles of domestic culture from the period in question, to gain inspiration for their competitative period exhibits

General definitions

Abstract   The innermost substance of a subject

Accessory   Anything apart from plant material used as part of a design

Arrangement   Another word for *Design* or *Exhibit*

Annual   Plant material that completes its cycle of growth in one year

Background   Any substance placed behind an exhibit of a complementary nature

Balance   Visual stability through an imaginary point of axis in an arrangement

Base   Any item on which the container stands

Basket   This must always be made of natural woven plant material

Best in show   An award given to the best of all first prize-winning exhibits

Bloom   A single flower or bud borne on a single stem

Bract   Classified as either flowers or foliage

Biennial   Plant material which completes its growth in two years

Bud   An unopened bloom not showing colour

Bulrush   Classified as both flower or seed-head

Candles   These are considered as accessories

Candlecups   These are considered part of a container

Collage   A selection of materials including plant life attached to a background

Coral   Including sea-fan and sea-fern. These are animal life and not plant material

Composition   An exhibit which includes the use of accessories

16

An Edwardian pewter tea-caddy combines with the soft peach tones
of Sonia roses and rosa rubrifolia foliage in this simple but effective
group

Collectors Corner
This magnificent antique copper kettle reflects the simple arrangement of a chrysanthemum spray, blackberries, ivy flowers and croton foliage. The completed design is enhanced by the orange velvet base

Condition   This refers to the state and quality of plant materials used in an exhibit at time of judging

Container   The receptacle which holds the plant material

Contemporary   Existing as of today

Design   Another word for *Exhibit* or *Arrangement*

Dinner table   An area of staging to be viewed from all sides and judged from a seated position

Disqualification   When an exhibitor does not comply with the schedule, eg the inclusion of artificial plant material, exceeding the stated measurements or using fresh plant life out of water-retaining substances

Distinction   Something which makes an exhibit outstanding

Drape   A piece of fabric used at the back of an exhibit or underneath. Drapes are not classified as accessories

Dried   This includes any natural dried, preserved, pressed, bleached or skeletonized material including wood

Driftwood   Any kind of natural dried wood which has been weathered by the elements including roots, branches or bark

Exhibit   Another word for *Design or Arrangement*. An exhibit is natural plant material with or without accessories

Exotic   Unusual greenhouse plant material

Figurine   Either one or a group used as a container or accessory

Flower   Any type of flower head on a single stem

Focal point   An area of interest in an exhibit

Foliage   The leafage of a plant of green buds not showing any colour

Fresh plant material   All living plant life

Fruit   Nuts, seed-heads, berries, gourds and cones, fungi and vegetables. Also all edible fruits. Rushes, reeds, grasses and cereals may be used as fruit

Garden plant material   Plant life which has been grown out of doors in Great Britain

Incorporate   To include

Interpretation   Correctly depicting the Class title in your own style

Landscape   An exhibit which depicts a naturalistic scene

Lichen   Natural plant life either fresh or dried

Line   Strong linear pattern or outline of an exhibit

Measurement   This always applies to the width, depth and height of the area allowed to stage an exhibit within

Mechanics   All aides by which plant material is contrived or supported

Miniature   An exhibit which is not more than 100 mm (4 in.) in any direction

Mobile   A hanging exhibit with free movement

Modern   An exhibit existing as of today in keeping with current décor

Moribana   A Japanese slyle exhibit in a shallow container

Natural plant material   Either fresh and/or dried

Niche   A recess in which an exhibit is placed for judging

Nagiere   A Japanese style exhibit of free-style in an upright container

Originality   Imaginative and inventive creativeness

Perennial   A plant that lives, blooms and sets seeds for more than two years

Pedestal   A stand, plinth or column on which a container is placed. It is always considered as part of the container

Period   An exhibit in keeping with a particular period in history

Petite   An exhibit which is more than 100 mm (4 in.) and less than 230 mm (9 in.) overall

Pot-et-fleur   Growing plants grouped with cut flowers within one container. Accessories may be used but not foliage

Predominate   A particular colour or type of flower used to a greater extent than other plant material in an exhibit

Proportion   The relationship between the plant material, container and space allocated

Rhythm   The use of plant material to illustrate movement and transition

Space   The overall area of staging in which to place an exhibit

Schedule   The exact details required for all classes in a show

Seaweed   This is a natural plant material

Swags   Also garlands – plant material must predominate

Texture   The tissue of plant material

Traditional   A style of flower arrangement which originated in a previous era and has been continually used

Variety   A named species, a hybrid or other development of a genus

Vertical   An upright exhibit

These definitions should be regarded only as a guide, they are not necessarily horticulturally correct, but should be acceptable to both exhibitors and judges at flower shows and flower arrangement competitions. Exhibitors should always remember that natural plant material must always predominate over everything else used in an exhibit. Living plant life must always be in water or some kind of water-retaining substance. This does exclude growing pot plants, fruits and vegetables. Artificially dyed or coloured plant material may be used unless the schedule states otherwise, but plastic or any other artificial plant life will cause disqualification.

Before entering any competition it is important to obtain an authorised list of standard definitions prepared by the organisation mentioned in the Schedule.

19

Preparation

It is much more difficult to arrange flowers at a show than it is at home. At home you are relaxed and inspiration often comes more easily when you are not watching the clock. At a show it is a different story. You only have a limited time to complete your exhibits and you will be dependent on the plant material you have taken with you. No chance to 'pop' into the garden for that extra sprig of foliage. A mock-up at home a day or two before the show is invaluable for finding flaws in your plan. When you practice, try to memorize the main placements of your design it is not necessary to use the exact plant materials for a mock-up, substitutes will show you the overall shape, colour and size.

Flowers should be ordered from the florist well in advance, stating varieties as well as colours. It is not always possible to get exactly the flower or colour you may want, so you should give alternatives as a second choice.

Gather outdoor plant material two days before the show either early in the morning or late evening when transpiration is at its lowest. Plant material in a winning exhibit must be fresh and unblemished. Select only crisp, fresh-looking material, removing any damaged leaves or flowers. Pick flowers in bud, re-cutting their stems under water to avoid air blockages. Leave them in deep cold water during conditioning, either in the light if you wish them to advance, or in the dark to retard their development. Leafy shrubs may be submerged under water overnight after crushing the woody stems. This does not include grey foliages which only require shallow water. All smooth surfaced leaves should be washed and dried, then rubbed over with a soft cloth dipped in olive oil. Remember all spring flowers have extra stored moisture in their stems so they only require shallow water. Roses picked in bud can be stored in a household refrigerator for up to six days if placed in a jar of water with their heads covered by a polythene bag. Peonies in bud can be retarded for as long as two weeks by sealing the ends of the stems with sealing wax and wrapping the flowers completely in metallic kitchen foil.

Place them on a cold stone floor until the day before the show, then re-cut the stems and place them in warm water and watch them burst open into perfect blooms.

Remember that the marquee or hall in which the show is held may be rather warm especially during the summer months, so make allowances for this when choosing your plant material.

Flowers may be transported to the show either in buckets of water weighted with pebbles in the bottom to give them stability, or packed in boxes lined with kitchen foil and surrounded by tissue paper to protect precious blooms.

Bases

These may be anything on which a container stands. They can be made of various substances such as slate, cork, marble, fabric covered boards, plates, trays, etc. They can also be of any colour, texture, size or shape but must be an integral component of the design, adding visual balance or artistic effect.

A base has the practical use of preventing polished furniture from becoming marked, as well as adding artistic effect for the finished design.

The simplest type of base can be made by covering a cake board with fabric. Round bases should be placed under curved containers, whereas square boards are ideal under oblong containers.

Judges will allocate marks for correct use of bases in relation to the overall finished design.

Containers

This is the definition used for any receptacle which holds the stem ends of flowers and foliage. They may or may not hold water. There are dozens of various shapes and designs including vases, bowls, troughs, urns, dishes, boxes, baskets, etc, all of which are used according to the style of arrangement required. Sometimes the container plays an important role in the overall design often being highly decorative and ornate. In other classes the container may be a simple dish or bowl which is completely hidden by the plant material. A class entitled *The Victorians* would call perhaps for a silver epergne or coloured glass compote, whereas another exhibit called *Vertigo* could use an empty coffee tin covered with adhesive fabric.

Shiny surfaced containers should not be filled entirely with flat surfaced materials but rather reflect the shine, by incorporating polished leaves or polished fruits.

Wooden or rough surfaced containers are ideal for dried preserved groups, and delicate fragile flowers such as lilies-of-the-valley, sweetpeas and miniature roses need the fine texture of porcelain to set them off. Figurines are very popular containers for show work but they should be used with care, as the physical lines of the figure always dictate the line of the flower arrangement.

Visual weight is another point to consider when choosing suitable containers for the plant material you wish to use. Do not overload statuettes with outstretched arms carrying flowers above their heads otherwise they will appear to be collapsing under the weight!

Containers which do not hold water may be lined with kitchen foil, or Oasis may be placed in a polythene bag and the flower stems pushed through the bag into the soaked foam.

A selection of useful containers for Show arrangements, include figures, pedestals, urns and bowls

Drapes

If you decide to use a drape to enhance your exhibit, then do make sure it is well pressed before hand. Roll the fabric on a cardboard tube to avoid creasing. Choose drapes with great care as their colour and texture can make or mar an arrangement. For example a shiny surfaced fabric such as satin or silk is often better placed with dull flat surfaced plant material, whilst textured linens provide stability to fragile flowers. Country style groups, using wild materials, or abstract and modern settings often require backgrounds of coarse fabric, such as hopsack or hessian.

Try to avoid patterned fabrics as these will confuse the overall composition.

Nets and tulle are only used when the schedule refers to ethereal type themes such as *Sleeping Beauty* or *Mid-Summer Night's Dream*.

The use of driftwood

Any piece of wood which has been weathered by the elements is known as driftwood, it does not have to have been washed up by the sea. The piece of wood may be a root, branch or stump and is always classified as plant material in the same way as leaves or flowers.

A walk through a country wood or along a remote beach will usually prove to be the best places for discovering driftwood. If you live in a city most good florists or garden centres sell pieces, but it is always more fun finding your own.

Pieces of wood invariably need cleaning, this can be done with hot water, household detergent and a scrubbing brush. After drying either in the sunshine or in front of a blower heater, the specimen will be ready for shaping. Seldom are pieces of driftwood found in perfect shape, most need some trimming with secateurs and a pointed knife to remove any soft wood. Wood that has been exposed to salt water and strong sunlight will be grey or even white in colour. Root stumps may be dark brown or even black if found in forests or dense undergrowth.

The very large pieces can be used as sculptural forms, slices of wood make excellent bases, branches provide interesting shapes for modern designs. Even small pieces can come in useful for hiding pinholders or mechanics.

Today

Here a modern arrangement uses a drain-pipe as a container. A plastic saucer is attached to the top to hold the Oasis in place.

Contorted driftwood gives diagonal line, and twisted cane adds movement to an essentially vertical design.

Six white carnations carefully placed add interest and impact to the focal area.

This exhibit would fit happily into any modern setting, and therefore aptly protrays the theme.

Modern designs rely on 'line' to convey their meaning. Judges will look for accurate placement of plant material. together with an overall feeling of unified movement within the finished exhibit.

When attempting modern arrangements remember simplicity is the essence of good design

What do judges look for?

Judges use accepted principles when judging flower arrangement classes at flower shows. These are:

Interpretation of the schedule

Basically, this means that the exhibit should interpret the wording of the schedule. A well designed arrangement with suitable flowers for the container must also illustrate by its shape, colour harmony, use of plant material or other factors, that which is required by the wording of the schedule.

Design

This is of great importance, as it means the overall picture, or impression, created with the materials you have chosen for a particular class. Individual components must be compatible and relate to each other, bearing in mind texture, shape and size; so that they unify and create the design required.

Scale

This not only means each piece of plant material should be related in size to the others, but also to the container and base, bearing in mind the size of the allocated space in the show. A good basic principle with vertical arrangements is that the plant material should be approximately one and a half times the height of the container. An arrangement in a shallow dish would be the same height as the length of the container. These are of course only guides, because often in modern or abstract designs more height is accepted if it is balanced with visual weight low down. Pretend that the space allowed on the staging is a frame and your arrangement should fit comfortably within it, with space to spare around the arrangement.

Balance

This category is divided into *Visual Balance* and *Actual Balance*. The first means that if an imaginary line was placed through the centre of the arrangement, each side should appear visually balanced, whether it be a symmetrical or asymmetrical design.

Symmetric designs have plant material equally placed on either side of the imaginary line. Asymmetric designs use lighter materials in the long side which are balanced with heavier larger and shorter flowers for the shorter side; this gives visual balance to the design. Actual balance is achieved by correct construction of the arrangement. Remember to place your first piece of foliage in an upright position at the back of the arrangement. Heavy rounded flowers should be used into the centre to give both visual and actual stability. Often exhibitors use small pieces of plumbers lead attached to the back rim of the container to help balance the design.

Colour

Judges should never show any personal preference for any particular colour harmony. However it is important for an exhibitor to fully interpretate what is required in the schedule with the use of colour. A good knowledge of the colour wheel will help. Orange, yellow and red are advancing colours while blue and violet recede. Green is neutral. Colours also appear 'light' or 'heavy' according to their tonal value. Pink is a tint and seems light in weight whereas maroon is a tone and looks heavy. Sometimes a Class in the schedule will require a specific colour harmony, eg an arrangement for a *Hot Summer Day* would call for something tranquil and cool in colour, whereas *Autumn Sunset* might incorporate glowing vibrant tones.

Suitability of plant material to container

The choice of container both in colour, texture, and size in relationship to the materials it holds is of great importance to the overall exhibit. Judges consider the container not for its individual beauty or intrinsic value but rather as a component of the completed design. Great care should be taken when choosing the plant material for a particular container to ensure that both colouring and plant tissue structure are in complete harmony.

Condition of plant material

It is important that an exhibitor checks the completed arrangement to make sure all natural plant material is either in water or water retaining foam. Judges will deduct points for faded, damaged or blemished blooms. Correct conditioning of plant material will ensure complete freshness throughout the period of the show.

Distinction and originality

In this section points are awarded for outstanding pieces of floral artistry. It could be the use of unusual plant material, or the clever use of familiar flowers and foliage. Perhaps a novel container, or unusual placement, even clever use of colour can provide distinctive effect.

Remember, distinction can only be achieved by original thought.

Technique and finish

Judges have keen eyes for discovering faults under this category. Often points are needlessly lost because of carelessness. Careful workmanship, sound construction, and neat finish, concealing the mechanics will avoid this. Do beware, however, the over-use of foliage to hide floral foam, as this can be considered wasteful. Marks will be gained by an exhibitor who has achieved the maximum visual effect from the materials used.

Farmhouse Kitchen
A weighing scale is the ideal container for this interpretative exhibit.
Parsnips, onions and mushrooms with sprays of blackberries, gold
freesia and chrysanthemums are arranged on one side to balance
the gourds on the other

Victoriana
A profusion of pink summer flowers gracefully cascade from this ·
silver epergne, perfectly portraying the theme

Colour harmonies
A glossary of terms used in floral art

Primary colours　Blue, yellow and red. These are pure
colours and cannot be made by compounding any other
colours

Secondary colours　Green, orange and violet are exact
intermediates between the primary colours. Green is a
mixture of blue and yellow; orange is a mixture of yellow
and red, and violet a mixture of red and blue

Tertiary colours　These are the exact intermediates between
primary and secondary colours, eg primary yellow,
secondary orange, tertiary tangerine

Tone　This describes how dark or light a colour is

Tint　Any colour lightened by the addition of white, eg a
tint of red would be pink

Shade　Any colour darkened by the addition of black,
eg a tone of red would be plum

Monochromatic　Shades, tints and tones of one colour only.
eg violet, lavender, lilac, purple

Polychromatic　Any number of colours selected at random
from the colour circle and used together, eg the Dutch
School of Flower Painting.

Complementary　Colours which lie opposite each other on
the colour circle and intensify each other when used
together, eg blue and orange

Adjacent　The most useful colour harmony and the easiest
to use. Colours which lie next to each other, but using
only one primary with a maximum of two others,
secondary or tertiary colours

Triadic　This is three colours equidistant apart on the
colour circle, eg yellow, red and blue. In flower
arranging it would be more attractive to use one of
these in great proportion to the other two.

The work of stewards

Stewards are appointed by the show committee to assist competitors in whatever way possible. They should always fully understand the wording of the schedule, because they are on duty during staging to help exhibitors, as well as during judging. It is advisable for the senior Steward to be an ex-exhibitor as she will then have an expert knowledge of all the problems which constantly face exhibitors.

A steward should know the number of entries in every class and where these are situated. Often several judges are appointed at larger shows and they only judge a few classes each, so they will have to be escorted on arrival by the steward to begin their work. Stewards should also know how many awards can be made, for they are responsible for completing the prizewinning cards after the judging. Only when a class has been completely judged should stewards affix the appropriate labels. Judges are highly sensitive people who prefer to work in complete silence, many stewards think this unsociable, but they should remain unobtrusive and only ask questions when judging is completed. Judges often wish to walk up and down to assess the overall standard of a class, stewards should not become their shadow, but remain static and attentive. It is not an easy job, but one which contributes a great deal to the success of judging. Most judges welcome questions from their steward after judging is finished. They will be only too pleased to explain any technical details.

Interpretative exhibits

Many schedules include special classes which ask the Exhibitor to interpret specific subject matter. An interpretative composite exhibit is the grouping together of unified items to make an overall pleasing picture. The exhibitor is aiming to compose a number of items, of which plant material must always predominate, to depict a particular theme. Each unit should be in complete harmony with the rest. It is always most interesting at a competitive flower show to see how several competitors interpret the same theme.

Always make a list of ideas associated with the subject. Use restraint in the number of items which you include in the finished composition. Understatement is often more effective than overstatement. Judges expect all components in the design to help interpret the subject.

The Apothecary

This class calls for an interpretative design using garden flowers, and herbs.

When arranging garden flowers remember their simplicity and keep the design as natural and free flowing as possible.

A stone bottle and mortar and pestle make suitable accessories for the theme.

Judges will appreciate carefully planned exhibits, and points are awarded for choice of accessories and their use, but remember they must never predominate over the plant material in the finished design

The use of accessories

When using accessories in an exhibit remember that they must never predominate in the overall design. Place your accessory in position before beginning the actual flower arrangement. The finished exhibit will include container, plant material, base and accessories which unify together to create the overall picture.

The base is very important, as it links the flower arrangement and accessories together. When more than one accessory is used in a design they are better grouped together, otherwise it gives an untidy haphazard effect. The accessory should be in scale with the other components, occupying no more than one third of the overall exhibit.

The facing photograph illustrates a large composite display, entitled '*A Marriage has been arranged*'.

Church pedestals comprise gladioli, chrysanthemums, dahlias, and longiflorum lilies,

Reception arrangements, include a Byzantine cone arrangement including single chrysanthemum spray and small bunches of green grapes.

Bridal bouquets, head-dresses, and corsages, provide foreground interest and complete the overall picture.

The background is effectively covered with a 'blow-up' version of the forthcoming marriages column of *The Daily Telegraph* newspaper.

The exhibit, by Howard Franklin, was awarded the Piggott Trophy, 1969, the Premier Award at Southport Flower Show

39

Styles for show arrangements

Traditional

This style applies to mass arrangements following either triangular or fan shaped outlines. The size can be anything from miniatures, to enormous church pedestal arrangements.

The container should be either urn shaped or a pedestal style, such as a candlestick.

A wide selection of plant material may be used of variety, shape and texture, although a closely related colour scheme is most usual.

The basic symetrical triangle often proves to be the most difficult, as it requires careful choice and placement of plant material.

The tallest piece of plant material should be one-and-half times the height of the container, and the width should be exactly the same as the height.

An urn is the best choice of container as it gives visual stability and balance.

The arrangement facing shows crown imperial lilies, longiflorum lilies, tulips, iris and carnations, boldly arranged with spring foliages, in a classical Grecian urn

40

Landscape

The exhibitor creates a natural scene, such as seashore, moorland or lakeside. It is a delightful style which relies on keen observation of nature. It is important to avoid man-made accessories as these destroy the naturalistic effect.

Plant material must always be in keeping with the scene portrayed. Containers are normally hidden, invariably shallow dishes or trays which make ideal receptacles for Landscape designs. The finished exhibit should appear realistic, with the plant material being used as it grows.

The Brontes

An intrepretative land-scape design, using grey slate as a base, and pieces of granite in the fore-ground.

Wild plant material is most suitable and includes heathers, ferns, ivy, and honeysuckle.

The arrangement is care-free and wind-swept, simply arranged in a concealed shallow dish.

The figures of the three Bronte sisters are made of *paper mâché* sculpture and give a sense of dramatic interest to the exhibit, as they battle against the wind across the moorland scene

Period

Every period of History has it own distinctive style, relying on decor and social conditions at the time. Whenever possible authentic containers should be used, or good reproduction styles.

Plant material and shape of the design must convey the atmosphere of the stated historical period. Exhibitors are advised to use their reference library for research before attempting Period pieces.

The Regency period is interpreted in this elegant design. Miniature roses, border carnations and sybil chrysanthemums are grouped around two bronze figurines, softened by a drape of chocolate brown silk

Abstract

This simply means using plant material in an unnaturalistic manner.

Decorative abstract is a pattern created with flowers, stems and leaves; using colour, texture and shape. The other style of abstract design is called 'expressive', which uses plant material to symbolize the essence of a subject, such as *Pride, Austerity, Fire or Age*.

Containers can be either simple geometric shapes or completely hidden in the case of expressive abstract designs.

Simplicity is essential in both abstract forms.

Black and White Construction
Arrangement by Edith Brack, using the stalks and ribs of the palmetto palm and the trimmed heads of the angelica, both painted black, highlighted with white swirling rattan

46

Modern

This is a category which is often referred to as 'free-form'. Dramatic effect, created with bold plant material following a strong linear pattern and emphasised by space within the design. Containers are usually hand-made pottery or glass, modern in shape and having a distinctive texture.

The Sculptor
A modern arrangement using three longiflorum lilies and two aralia leaves. Driftwood and stone give dramatic effect to this distinctive design

Exotic East

The inscrutable face of the Orient is portrayed with this simple design of three anthurium lilies, and fatsia foliage, thoughtfully placed in a well pin-holder, on a wooden cork base. The mechanics have been hidden with the use of a piece of fungus. The curving stems and form of the anthurium flowers in conjunction with the pointed outlines of the foliage convey the refinement of oriental culture.

The very nature and substance of the plant material used aptly imparts to the judge it's true meaning, without the use of any accessories, which would clutter and distract from the aesthetic quality of the design

Mystery of the Orient

A moribana exhibit using a shallow container in the Japanese style.

A single stem of limelight lilies is balanced at the base of the design by magasea leaves.

The pin-holder which holds the plant material in position is concealed by an attractive piece of stone.

A figurine of a goddess compliments the design, and adds fore-ground interest.

Simplicity is the essence of good Oriental style arranging. A feeling of space surrounding each individual flower helps to convey the theme.

The Japanese name for these lilies is Hime-yuri, they are traditionally used only for special celebrations during the month of May.

The arrangement of flowers has always been regarded in Japan as an occupation befitting learned men, priests, philosophers, and men of rank have been it's most enthusiastic followers.

Various rules are observed as to the use of water in flower containers.

In spring and autumn the vase should be nine-tenths filled, in summer nearly full, whereas in winter the container should only be four-fifths full. It is important to note that the surface of the water in which the flowers are placed is technically regarded as the soil from which the arrangement grows.

The arranger must convey the impression of stable origin in the design

Geometric

Many different outline shapes make up this section. Including Crescent, Hogarth Curve, Vertical, Horizontal and Diagonal. Most geometric shapes can be easily formed with plant material. It is advisable to only use the minimum amount of varieties as this gives a clearer effect. Larger rounded flowers are used at the centre of interest with smaller plant material at the extremities. Exhibitors should remember that the space surrounding the outline of a geometric design is all important for its visual clarity.

OVERLEAF
An Italian alabaster pillar makes a perfect base for a buffet table arrangement.

Ranunculas, freesia, and roses, together with damson blossom are arranged in a casual, informal style. They are sufficiently raised above table level to comply with judging regulations, for this style of design

Quince, cymbidium orchids, Belinda roses, and freesia, are elegant flowers for a downward sweeping crescent design in an antique pedestal container

Coalbrookdale cast iron urn holds a miscellany of late summer
flowers arranged in a traditional style

The Mariner

The interpretation of this theme has been carefully thought out with clever use of a fabric drape representing not only the ship's mast and sail in the background, but also the waves of the sea flowing across the base.

Longiflorum lilies with their finely sculptured form portray strength and stability of character, and give dramatic impact to the design. Careful use of senecio greyii and eucalyptus foliage adds movement together with good colour harmony in relation to the drape.

A bronze figure of the Mariner gazes across the arrangement as if looking from the ship's bow and out to the open sea. The upright form of the figure gives further visual stength to the overall exhibit

59

South Pacific

Another interpretative design using a carved wooden face mask in the central focal area.

Eremurus is used for back-ground height, although these could easily be substituted with either delphiniums or gladioli.

Exotic tiger lilies, carnations, croton foliage, and caladium leaves are dramitically grouped around the mask.

Foreground interest is provided with lotus seed heads, coconuts, and bananas, which complete the tropical scene.

The finished design is displayed on a hession covered board.

When attempting to enter this type of schedule class research must be done to discover and obtain the correct exotic material with which to depict the scene

The prophet Isaiah said *The Glory of Lebanon shall come upon thee, the fir tree, the pine tree, and the box together, to beautify the place of my Sanctuary.*

Today's flower arrangers continue the ancient tradition of beautifying our religious buildings with magnificent displays of flowers.

Care should be taken to use the correct liturgical colour schemes according to the Church's calendar. Yellow and white for Easter symbolising glory and perfection. All white for Christmas, and all red forWhitsuntide, prepresenting the tonques of fire at Pentecost. Red is also used on Saints Days, and in remembrance of the blood shed by the holy martyrs. All green foliage arrangements are most effective during the Sundays in Trinty. Most churches remain un-decorated during Lent and also Advent.

Large symmetrical triangular designs, as illustrated, show up well even from the back of the church.

Gladioli, carnations, rudbeckia, and longiflorum lilies are sufficiently bold shapes for this kind of design.

A stone garden figure makes a suitably stable container blending perfectly with the majesty of a church interior

A church arrangement of summer garden flowers arranged in a stone garden figurine

Table decorations

The shape and size of the table will naturally suggest the shape of the floral design.

Low arrangements are most suitable for dinner tables, as it is important for guests at a dinner party to be able to see each other across the table. Whereas buffet table arrangements should be raised off the table as guests are normally standing and the design should never interfere with the dishes of food.

Judges are seated to judge dinner table arrangements and standing for buffet table exhibits. They will take into account the colour and choice of napery and china if used. Schedules are always definite in their requirements regarding accessories in table decoration classes.

Dinner Party
A triangular container makes a different base for this traditional table arrangement of tigrum lilies, evergold roses and apricot freesia. Slender taper candles complete the arrangement

Duo
Complementary arrangements of longiflorum lilies, buddleia, rudbeckia, anthruium lilies and roses are linked together with a flowing drape of satin fabric

Petite arrangements should be larger than 102 mm, but less than 229 mm, overall.

Here, a fine white porcelain cherub, seated upon a dolphin, supports a delicate group of helibores, border carnations, grape hyacinths, and prunus.

The design is arranged on a horizontal plane bearing in mind the limitations on size. Only small flowers are used, otherwise the cherub would appear overladen, and unbalanced. Buds and pointed shapes of plant material are kept to the perimeter of the design, whereas the rounded floral shapes are effectively grouped into the focal area

Pot-et-fleur

An ever increasing interest in indoor house plants has prompted flower shows to include *pot-et-fleur* Classes in most schedules. It means growing plants grouped together in one container together with cut flowers. The container or bowl must be suitable to hold enough compost for the roots of the plants and they must be chosen so as to live happily together in the same environment. The cut flowers are arranged in a piece of water retaining foam placed into another hidden container within the bowl, concealed by moss or the plants themselves. Exhibitors must remember that cut foliage must not be used in *pot-et-fleur* arrangements.

Compatibility
Growing plants and cut flowers, living together in unity.
    Award winning design at the National Competition organised by The National Association of Flower Arrangement Societies in 1975.
designed by Mrs W Wilsher, from Devon
Photograph by courtesy of the Flowers Publicity Council

Floral design for exhibition

Flower festivals

Not every flower arranger wishes to compete for awards or prizes in competitive classes at flower shows, they may prefer to exhibit their designs just for visual pleasure.

Flower festivals provide the ideal opportunity for doing distinctive design work in beautiful settings.

Most flower festivals are held either in churches or stately homes, as these present decorative features which dictate the style, mood and colour of the various arrangements.

When arranging flowers in churches particular note should be taken of the memorials, statues, stained glass windows, altar frontals and period of the building, bearing in mind scale in proportion to the building. Flowers should enhance the existing features of the church and never try to hide or out-do them.

Flower festivals should have an overall director who plans the entire scheme of flower arrangements, their shape, size, colour and placement. The work is carried out by a team of talented arrangers who are able through their expertise to follow the instructions and plan of the director. Often a theme is required, perhaps a hymn title or quotation from the Bible to be portrayed in plant material. This calls for careful planning and research by the arrangers so the finished pieces perfectly fit the theme.

Colour grouping in blocks of colour creates impact and arrests the eye. The sanctuary could be gloriously displayed with crashing reds and purples, matching an altar frontal used for saints days in crimson brocade. Blue hues together with lime green foliages would be perfect for a Lady Chapel. The main nave area and side windows a radiant glow of apricot and yellow tones with the baptistry decorated in pure white using fragile and sweet scented blooms, representing child-hood.

Every church presents its own special problems. It could be high or sloping window sills, over colourful stained glass windows or even a lack of natural daylight. All these and other similar problems can be overcome with careful thought by the director and his team. Flower festivals have a duration of three to four days, so flowers and foliage must be chosen with good lasting qualities, because spectators viewing on the final day will still expect to see them in perfect condition.

Daily watering, and atomizing with a sprayer of water early in the morning and again at dusk will be sufficient to keep everything looking fresh. Remember that if you are invited to take part in a Flower Festival, you are one of a team and that the finished overall decoration must appear unified as a whole. Individual arrangements may have their own distinctive features but they also must link together to form the completed scheme of decor.

Working together with other floral artists can be a most rewarding experience, but do not try to out-do your neighbour as in competition work, otherwise all the joy and pleasure of team effort will be lost. Church flower festivals are to the glory and praise of God and not the arrangers.

Avenue of Peace
Festival of flowers at Westminster Cathedral 1977. Arranged
by the Dutch Flower Growers' Association.

OPPOSITE
Pedestal arrangement for Winchester Cathedral by Julia
Clements using dry palmetto leaves and pampas grass with
acanthus to form the outline of the design, with fresh
flowers in the centre.

72

Show themes and suggestions for classes

Most large flower shows and national competitions take an overall theme for the Floral Art section. This is used as the inspiration for the various classes. Here are some suggestions.

OVERALL THEME	**A World of Flowers**
Class 1	*The Common Market* A window display of exhibitors own choice to depict the theme
Class 2	*Far Away Places* An exhibit representing aspects of a country to be named, open only to flower clubs
Class 3	*Ancient Egypt* An exhibit of natural dried plant material
Class 4	*United Nations* A pedestal arrangement in polychromatic colour harmony
Class 5	*Bon Voyage* Pot-et-fleur suitable for a ships cabin, on a long voyage
Class 6	*Mystery of the Orient* A moribana exhibit depicting the Far East

OVERALL THEME	**Literary Scene**
Class 1	*The Classics* An interpretative design open only to Flower Clubs
Class 2	*Nobel Prize* A pedestal arrangement using natural foliage only
Class 3	*Poets Corner* An exhibit to interpret a quotation to be named, using natural plant material
Class 4	*Green Mantle* An exhibit of green fresh plant material
Class 5	*New Release* A modern design using natural plant material
Class 6	*Fictional Character* An interpretative design using natural plant material

OVERALL THEME	**Our Heritage**
Class 1	*In the Beginning* An abstract design
Class 2	*Cardinal Wolsey* An interpretative exhibit using red colourings only
Class 3	*Edwardian Elegance* A pedestal arrangement. Fresh plant material to predominate
Class 4	*Master Crafts* A design using fresh plant material depicting a craft to be named
Class 5	*Nostalgia* An exhibit to depict an historical period, using fresh plant material only
Class 6	*Burns Night* An exhibit for a Burns' Night Dinner table using fresh plant material.

Other specifications would be given in an actual schedule. Namely the dimensions of each class area, dates and times for staging exhibits, also the colouring of the staging backcloth and of course the prize money.

When drawing up a show schedule it is advisable to bear in mind the time of the year it is to be held. For instance all foliage arrangements are difficult in springtime but simple in summer. Grandiose pedestals would be expensive to arrange in winter but again very suitable for summer shows.

The schedule committee has a very important task because their planning and imagination has to stimulate the creative minds of the exhibitors who make the show a success.

Training classes, schools and opportunities

Florists and flower arrangers

Floristry is a highly artistic profession as a means of livelihood. It normally takes six years to qualify as a skilled florist. All floristry examinations in the United Kingdom of Great Britain are conducted by The Society of Floristry. There are three preliminary examinations Stages I, II and III, an Intermediate Certificate and the National Diploma. Flower arrangers, on the other hand are not normally considered to be professionals, as their main object is the arrangement of cut flowers and foliage for artistic effect and personal pleasure. Some flower arrangers, however, become extremely proficient and also qualify, by sitting the City and Guilds examinations in Flower Arrangement, after following courses in colleges of adult education.

Training classes

Classes in Floristry and Flower Arrangement are held at numerous colleges of further education throughout Great Britain. These lead to recognized examinations and successful students receive graded certificates and qualifications.

Information regarding courses can be obtained from your local college or the *Education Officer* at the *County Hall* or a library.

Schools

Numerous private schools exist for both flower arrangement and floristry. Many of them offer intensive training, also their own certificates and diplomas. Further particulars regarding duration of courses, fees and residential facilities should be obtained by contacting them directly. Information regarding private schools may be obtained from *British Retail Flower Association, 281 Flower Market, New Covent Garden, London SW8. Telephone 01–720 8418.*

76

Two young students busily working on their designs for City
and Guilds examinations

Opportunities

After completing a course in Floristry, there are ample openings for an enthusiastic Florist, either by starting their own business or working for existing companies in retail trading, contract work or hotel décor. The work is varied and interesting, never boring or repetitious, with an opportunity for self expression and artistic creativity.

Flower arrangers when proficient can compete in flower shows, arrange church flower festivals, or even undertake floral decorations for dances and parties. Some flower arrangers continue their training and become teachers, demonstrators, lecturers or judges of floral art. This can take them around the country and sometimes even abroad on assignments at flower shows and flower clubs. At national level eminent flower arrangers command high professional fees for their work which can become a fulltime occupation.

Organizations

The National Association of Flower Arrangement Societies of Great Britain (NAFAS)
21A Denbigh Street
London SW1
Telephone   01–828 5145
For information regarding flower clubs, demonstrators, lectures and judges throughout the United Kingdom of Great Britain and the Republic of Eire.

The Society of Floristry
The Hon Secretary
Mrs Shirley Ake, SFDip
44 Rossett Avenue
Harrogate, Yorkshire
The National Examining Body for Professional Floristry Qualifications in Great Britain. Also information regarding judges and demonstrators.

The Royal Horticultural Society
Vincent Square
London SW1
Telephone 01–834 4333
Membership includes entrance to Chelsea Flower Show and a monthly magazine.

Magazines

The Flower Arranger
A quarterly publication, annual subscription including postage £2.00 mailed to an address in the United Kingdom of Great Britain.
Further details from
Taylor Bloxham Ltd
Tyrrell Street
Leicester

The Florist Trade Magazine
Monthly magazine for professional florists, annual subscription £4.00 including postage mailed anywhere in Great Britain.
Further details
The Florist
120 Lower Ham Road
Kingston, Surrey

Flora Magazine
Bi-monthly magazine for flower arrangers and gardeners. Annual subscription £4.00 including postage mailed anywhere in Great Britain.
Further details
Stanley Gibbons Magazines Ltd,
Drury House
Russell Street
London WC2

Educational leaflets

The National Association of Flower Arrangement Societies of Great Britain, 21A Denbigh Street, London SW1 *Telephone* 01−828 5145 produce excellent leaflets on Basic Equipment Preserving Plant Material, Drying Plant Material, Use of Driftwood, Pressed Flower Pictures, Home made Containers, and others at a cost of 10p each plus 10p for postage and packing.

Flowers Publicity Council, Agriculture House, Knightsbridge, London SW1 *Telephone* 01−235 4706 produce four free leaflets on Care of House Plants, Care of Cut Flowers, Guide to Flower Arranging and Flowers of the Zodiac. Enclose 10p stamp to cover postage.
They also have a weekly telephone service. By dialling 01−499 4191 you can hear a recorded message of best buys of flowers and plants and information on their care.

The Society of Floristry
Hon Secretary, Mrs Shirley Ake
44 Rossett Avenue
Harrogate, Yorkshire
Supply various leaflets on all aspects of professional floristry − write for further details.

City and Guilds of London Institute
46 Britannia Street
London, WC1
Telephone 01−278 2468
The National Examining Body for Flower Arrangement Qualifications in Great Britain

National Council of State Garden Clubs Inc (USA)
4401 Magnolia Avenue
St Louis
Missouri 63110 USA
For information regarding Flower and Garden Clubs in the
United States of America.

Flowers Publicity Council
Agriculture House
Knightsbridge
London, SW1
Telephone   01–235 4706
Comprises Growers, Wholesalers and Florists of Britains
Commercial flower industry.

Interflora
Interflora House
Sleaford
Lincolnshire
Telephone   0529–304141
World-wide Flower Relay Organisation of Professional
Florists, Judges and Demonstrators.

A view of the author's studio showing a selection of summer
flowers in the foreground and a range of floral art containers
behind

Metric Equivalent Table — approximate

1 inch	–	25 mm
2 inches	–	50 mm
3 inches	–	75 mm
4 inches	–	100 mm
5 inches	–	125 mm
6 inches	–	150 mm
7 inches	–	175 mm
8 inches	–	200 mm
9 inches	–	230 mm
10 inches	–	255 mm
11 inches	–	280 mm
12 inches	–	305 mm
2 feet	–	60 cm
3 feet	–	90 cm
4 feet	–	120 cm
5 feet	–	150 cm
6 feet	–	180 cm

Florists' flowers

Always buy your flowers from a reputable florist, it is a short sighted policy to buy from street stalls or market traders as the conditions their flowers have been kept in will not be ideal and thereby shorten their lives. Florists flowers are especially grown for their long lasting qualities and they can be relied upon even under show conditions. Make sure that the foliage is firm and green and that when removed from the shop vase the stems also appear to be green in colour not brown or slimy.

Roses — top ten

1   *Baccarat*   brilliant red
2   *Forever Yours*   crimson
3   *Pink Sensation*   mauvy pink
4   *Belinda*   vibrant orange small in size
5   *Evergold*   true yellow small in size
6   *Roselandia*   old fashioned tea-rose
7   *Carole*   miniature pink
8   *Tiara*   delightful small pure white
9   *Sonia*   soft peach full petals
10 *Dr Verhauge*   antique gold

Florists' roses should have their thorns removed, the stems should be cut with a slanting cut and also split up the stem. The ends of the stems are placed in shallow boiling water for fifteen seconds and then into a bucket of deep cold water. This releases any air blockages in the stem and avoids the heads bending or drooping at the neck.

Carnations – top ten

1 *Arthur Sim*   white with red tips
2 *Blue Sydney*   lilac
3 *Clove*   crimson red
4 *Dusty Sim*   old rose pink
5 *Harvest Moon*   creamy gold
6 *Laddie Sim*   salmon pink
7 *Lolita*   shocking pink
8 *Midas*   clear yellow
9 *Snow Maiden*   pure white
10 *William Sim*   bright red

Carnations are always conditioned by placing them in a container of 'fizzy' lemonade before arranging. They should also be atomized with water onto their petals.

American all-the-year-around chrysanthemum sprays

1 *Apricot Marble*   single soft peach
2 *Blue Chip*   lilac pink double
3 *Dragon*   deep bronze double
4 *Elegance*   white or primrose double
5 *Galaxy*   single bronze, gold or yellow
6 *Hayday*   deep yellow double
7 *Inferno*   russet single
8 *Matador*   deep bronze anemone centre
9 *Portrait*   soft pink double
10 *Tuneful*   orange or bronze single

Chrysanthemums need plenty of deep water for conditioning and should not be crowded together otherwise the petals will become damaged and fall. Stems should be split upwards never crushed.

Lilies — top ten

1   *Arum*   available in spring white in colour
2   *Auratum*   available mid-summer, white trumpet
flowers with yellow mark and crimson spots
3   *Candidum*   early summer, the Madonna lily, pure white
trumpets
4   *Cernuam*   mid-summer. Dainty pink flowers spotted
purple
5   *Henryi*   Autumn availability, deep orange/yellow
spotted brown
6   *Longiflorum*   available from spring through to autumn.
The true Easter lily. Large white trumpet flowers
7   *Regale*   available mid-summer, yellowish-white
flowers with exterior red shading
8   *Rubrum*   available in summer. White trumpet flowers
with deep crimson backs
9   *Tigrum*   all year around, bright orange spotted black
10 *Umbellatum*   summertime — brilliant orange, spotted
dark crimson.

Remove the anthers with flowers scissors otherwise the pollen
will stain fabrics.

Flower arrangement judging table

	Maximum points
Interpretation of the Schedule	20
Design	20
Colour harmony	20
Technique, economy and condition of plant material	20
Distinction	20
Maximum points	100

Judges use judging tables to enable them to allocate marks under various headings which ensures a completely un-biased and fair judgement.

Garden trees and shrubs

My choice of useful trees and shrubs for show arrangements easily grown in your own garden

Acer campestre   Shining maroon foliage which turns golden red in the autumn

Alnus incana 'Aurea'   Golden leaved alder most attractive in both spring and summer. In winter the stems are a showy red

Aucuba japonica 'Variegata'   The variegated laurel. Glossy green leaves mottled with gold

Berberis 'thunbergii   Pale yellow flowers in the spring. Brilliant foliage and red fruit in the autumn

Cupressus plumosa 'Aurea'   Slow growing with bright yellow foliage

Elaeagnus pungens 'Aureo Variegata'   Golden yellow evergreen foliage, particularly bright in winter

Euonymus europaeus   Brilliant autumn hues of the foliage. Large red fruits open to show attractive orange seeds

Garrya elliptica   Evergreen, with long grey-green catkins produced on male plants early in the year

Gingko biloba   Beautiful yellow tinted autumn foliage, known as the maidenhair tree

Hedra dentata 'Aurea'   Large leaved variegated ivy

Liriodendron tulipifera   The tulip tree is valued for its tulip-like greenish white flowers, also attractive foliage which turns deep yellow at the end of the year

89

Mahonia bealei   Handsome pinnate rich green foliage, with delightful lily-of-the-valley. Yellow scented flowers in winter

Perowskia atriplicifolia   Grey aromatic foliage, a truly beautiful shrub

Pieris forrestii   Brilliant scarlet young foliage contrast with dark green mature leaves

Prunus cerasifera 'Bleirana'   Rich bronze foliage throughout the summer and rose pink blossom in March

Quercus coccinea   Handsome foliage until the end of November, commonly known as scarlet oak.

Rhus cotinus   Dramatic purple foliage

Senecio greyii   Long sprays of silver foliage all year round

Viburnum fragrans   Pale pink buds which open into white scented flowers, followed by scarlet berries. Flowers from November

Weigela florida Foliis Purpureis   Purplish foliage and rose pink flowers which appear in June

Hardy perennials

*My choice of hardy perennials which can be grown outdoors
and will continue to grow for many years, producing endless
flowers and foliage for your show arrangements*

Acanthus spinosus   Purplish flowers and attractive arching
foliage needs shade and good drainage

Achillea filipendulina Eupatorium   Feathery green foliage and
handsome flat yellow flower heads like a golden plate.
Sunny position

Astilbe Japonica   Elegant pink, red or white flowers, feathery
in appearance, need damp position

Bergenia cordifolia   Evergreen leathery foliage grows well
in shade. Clustered deep pink flower heads open in
February. Foliage turns deep pink in autumn

Cephalaria tartarica   Tall yellow scabious lasts well as a cut
flower. Requires rich soil.

Delphinium   Popular tall spiked flowers, in June and July.
Pacific Giant strain excellent for pedestal groups

Eryngium oliverianum   The sea holly has deep blue heads,
with white veined green leaves. May be used fresh or
dried and is most decorative

Helleborus orientalis   The lenten rose, flowers from
February onwards. Beautiful spotted crimson and maroon,
with green flushings

Heuchera   Graceful flowers in June and July, with broad
leaves usually a coppery-mahogany colour. They like
plenty of sunshine

Hosta crispula   Formerly known as funkia the leaves have an appealing crinkly white edge to them. Prefers a shady moist position

Iris foetidissima   Flourishes almost anywhere. Beautiful purple flowers, grey-green foliage and seed pods which when split reveal showy orange seeds

Kniphofia galpinii   Red hot pokers flowering from July to October. Orange-apricot flowers which are useful in large pedestal arrangements

Ligularia clivorum   Vivid daisy flowers during July and August. Beautiful large leathery dark green leaves often used in foliage arrangements

Lupinus   Modern lupins are available in a tremendous colour range. They should be cut as soon as the lower florets open in late May or early June

Macleaya cordata   Pearly white plume poppy, superb for cutting, requires partial shade

Paeonia lactiflora   The sweet scented double Chinese paeony. Flowers should be cut in bud and placed in deep water

Penstemon barbatus   Scarlet tubular flowers throughout the whole summer. A light soil and plenty of sunshine are their only requirements

Physalis gigantea   Cape gooseberry often called Chinese lanterns. Ideal for drying for winter decoration

Polygonatum multiflorum   The Solomon's seal produces beautiful arching foliage with hanging tubular white flowers often flushed with green. It requires a shady spot under trees

Rodgersia pinnata Superba   Tall spikes of pink flowers, coppery coloured seed pods in autumn. Handsome foliage which turns chestnut red in late summer

Thalictrum dipterocarpum   This should be in every flower arrangers garden as it produces beautiful lilac flowers and distinctive feathery foliage.

Suppliers — top ten

1	*Bulbs*	Van Tubergen Ltd
		Willow Bank Wharf
		Ranelagh Gardens
		London, SW 6
		Telephone 01–736 2313
2	*Ferns*	Reginald Kaye Ltd
		Waithman Nurseries
		Silverdale
		Carnforth, Lancashire
		Telephone 0524–701252
3	*Florists*	K B M Shirley Co Ltd
	cut flowers	306 Flower Market
	(wholesale)	New Covent Garden
		Nine Elms, London, SW8
		Telephone 01–720 7129
4	*House plants*	Thomas Rochford
		Turnford Hall Nurseries
		Broxbourne
		Hertfordshire
		Telephone 61–64512
5	*Perennials*	Treasures Ltd
		Tenbury Wells
		Worcestershire
		Telephone 0584–810777
6	*Roses*	Le Grice Roses Ltd
		Roseland Nurseries
		North Walsham
		Norfolk
		Telephone 06924–2591
7	*Seeds*	Thompson & Morgan Ltd
		London Road
		Ipswich
		Suffolk
		Telephone 0473–214226

8	*Sundries*	Douthwaite Florists
	Dried materials	Sundries Ltd
	Containers etc	Donisthorpe Street
	(wholesale)	Leeds 10
		Telephone 0532–450894
9	*Trees and shrubs*	Hillier and Sons
		Winchester
		Hampshire
		Telephone 0962–69245
10	*Films and slides*	Gerard Holdsworth
		Productions Ltd
		31 Palace Street
		London, SW1
		Telephone 01–828 1671

Bibliography

Flowers in Church, Jean Taylor, Mowbrays
Excellent publication covering all aspects of the subject

Flower Arranging in House and Garden, George Smith,
Pelham Books
Beautifully presented arrangements, and informative text
on the cultivation of interesting garden plants

Flower Arranging, Michael Goulding,Ward Lock
A professional London Florist's advice on Floral Art

Flower Craft, Violet Stephenson, Hamlyn
A facinating miscellany of floral ideas

Floral Art, Betty Stockwell, FrederickWarne
Original ideas on Modern and Abstract flower arrangement

Flowers in Praise, Julia Clements, Batsford
Useful picture book of church decoration

The ABC of Flower Arranging, Julia Clements, Batsford
A step-by-step approach for beginners

Flower Arranging from your Garden, Sheila Macqueen,
Delightful book following the traditions of the late
Constance Spry

Garden Foliage for Flower Arrangement, Sibyl Emberton,
Faber
A must for every flower arrangers book-shelf

The art of Japanese Flower Arranging, Stella Coe,
Barrie and Jenkins
The best guide book to Eastern style (Ikebana) floral
arrangement